AF317029

THE PARENT SQUAD

Dr. Ruth Doriscar-Cook
The Parent Squad

Published by Spines
ISBN 979-8-89691-785-4

THE PARENT SQUAD

KEY PRACTICES TO RAISING OUR CHILDREN IN THIS SOCIETY

DR. RUTH DORISCAR-COOK

CONTENTS

INTRODUCTION

This book provides key practices that can be applied in your way using examples that I've experienced personally or witnessed and intervened in professionally as a social worker. As society changes, so does the way we parent. There is a slight shift that has been lost in the "fad of life" and the lack of balance in our lives. So, as we go through the motions of providing for our children, we must uphold certain values that help us maintain our parenting responsibilities that affect us all. We can't always control who our child goes to school with (unless home-schooled) or who our child eventually has contact with; so indeed, bad parenting eventually affects us all, and so does good parenting. This book is not to measure your parenting skills but more of a way for you to add some methods to your parenting journey. Keep in mind that there are different reasons why, even if you do your best, there will be things outside of your control.

For one thing, nature-nurture theory is a venture that will eventually be known as your child grows. Genetic dispositions and the environment can seem to clash even when all children are raised in the same environment. They may view things differently because they are affected differently. Sociology and psychology also have the birth order theory that continues to be researched. Many variables affect our family unit because as we raise our kids, we tend to grow and learn from those parenting experiences. It's important to take note of those lessons as we experience them. It's things like this diaper commercial always makes me laugh. It indicates how with your 1st kid, you buy the most expensive brand of diapers, and you're the extreme germaphobe protecting that child, and then you have the 2nd kid, and you get over it! This happens because we grow with experience. We realized in that situation that no matter how hard we tried, that child still "caught a cold," and we also noticed that when we didn't try, the child did not "catch a cold" or even crazier, the 2nd child didn't catch a cold at all, and it wasn't really because of the effort we took because quite possibly we just didn't have the time to clean as well as we did with one child. The point is, this book will provide you with illustrations, and some steps to guide you, and help you through the challenges of raising that child or children of yours. And hopefully, you will not feel alone on this journey of parenting.

It doesn't matter how you became a parent; the fact is you are, and it started in the womb when you heard your baby's heartbeat in the womb, and you, as well as your loved ones, started taking precautions with you. Whether you're a father or a mother, you are now part of the parenting squad. Within this squad are different categories based on your personal life condition. But no matter the conditions, the responsibility to parent your child or children is yours. In this parenting process, you'll find yourself parenting other people's kids as well at times, if for nothing else but to encourage good behaviors around your child. This means parenting can also begin with an assignment, whether it is fostering or adopting, marrying someone with a child or children, or inheriting a child or children. This can occur because of family members who are in prison or have died, or maybe you found a child who is not being taken care of as well, and you are now stepping in to assist where the parents cannot. I welcome you to the parenting squad. Just so you know, that old saying "We want to have children to get it out of the way"? Well, the only thing you can get out of the way is pregnancy. "Getting a child or children out of the way" is not accurate because parenting is a lifelong journey and technically a lifetime worry, as well as responsibility for life. Even if your child is the best child ever, a parent's heart will always want to take that charge, and you will always have concerns about the livelihood and life of your child or children. However, your parenting journey does start; know that there will be layers to unpack. We are in a life that is always shifting. So, let us begin to unpack these layers of raising that child or children of yours.

CHAPTER ONE

PARENTING IS A JOURNEY

ONE
PARENTING IS A JOURNEY

The beginning layers of parenting can be led by instinct. Most of us have protective instincts that will now multiply by an infinite number. After preparing for the baby to come home in a safe and clean environment, your protective instincts will cause you to make sure your baby is breathing while he or she is sleeping peacefully. Then, once you hear the baby crying, you quickly rush to make sure your baby is safe. It doesn't matter if all the infant wants is your touch or presence. Either way, you are content knowing your baby is safe. If you do not have enough of a protective instinct to be left alone with your baby or babies, simply seek out help.

The parenting journey is as long as your child/children are alive. They will always need you. As mentioned in the introduction, there is no such thing as having children to get it over with because as your child (ren) develops, the need for you may change, but they'll always need mom and dad for life. As long as you understand, just because your child needs something different from you does not mean you are not just as essential in their lives as you were when you were changing their diapers. The confusing part of it is your child may think they don't need you and have it all figured out, but this is when you have to wisely step in and show them mommy/daddy can help or get help for this new season of their lives too. For this chapter, the focus is on keeping up with your child as his or her needs change and not allowing it to drive you crazy, at least not off any ledge.

I recall when I was about 14 years old, my brother and I would get picked up from school by our mom, who would run her errands with us. Although it was her usual thing to do, at that moment, all I could recall was being so frustrated that day. So, as the assertive child out of my mother's 4 children, I asked her, "Mommy, why can we just go home after school?" Her response was as surprising to me as my question was to her… "Because you all always beg me to take you out by crying and whining," saying, "Mommy, don't go home now." As my memory of what she stated served me well, I soaked it up and went along with it for now. My mother quickly realized she would now run most of her errands before picking us up or have my father do it as she ran her necessary errands, or at times, just deal with my teenage moodiness until I adjusted. In my case, I started reading books even more when I felt bored with all of my mother's errands. My point is my interest changed, and as a teenager, I did not even realize our mother was accommodating our needs initially. My mother reminding me was the best thing she could have done for my peace of mind because it reduced my annoyance immediately. As a teenager back then, without the innovation of cell phones (or it may have been too expensive for us at the time), all I wanted was to probably hurry home to get on our landline phone with my friends. Today, children have a variety of items such as tablets, phones, headsets and laptops to distract them from the boredom of being with a parent taking care of business, but my mother curtailed my negative responses by communicating how this was what we originally wanted at first, and that was to run errands with her. As hormones and developmental changes occur in kids, they end up wanting different things, and it is up to the parent(s) to pay attention and highlight those transitions in order to limit your frustrations with your child's development. This is part of the journey to parenting. Social development can take parents by surprise, but children are not aware that their constant growth can impact us emotionally and financially, among other things too. They don't even realize their own social development as a thing because it is normal for them. For example, my daughter used to get her hair braided with her father at the age of 8 years old. The braids were simple enough; they were just back braids. I recall how offended my husband used to get when she started missing their Saturday hair appointment rituals. At this time, she was almost 13 years old, and it just was not that important to her anymore. After about a month of it becoming my responsibility to do her hair (hint) now, I was near frustration, so I confronted her as casually and as suggestively as I possibly could. Asking, "Why aren't you getting your hair done with daddy anymore?" She looked at me with apologetic eyes, saying, "Mommy, I don't like how I look anymore in that style. Some people thought I was gay." Well, I still busted into laughter because her concerns were surprising to me. Yes, I understand she had social concerns prior, but we had not talked about them on the scale of how her appearance would have impacted her behavior. My daughter and I have had open communication about her attractions since she was 6 years old. I mean, it is as open as it could be between a 6-year-old child and a mother. This occurred because of this incident with an outfit and my inquisitiveness as a parent; in other words, I was nosy. At the time, my daughter was 6 years old in a Tommy Hilfiger jumpsuit that we loved, but all of a sudden, she refused to wear it to school. When I asked, she said, "There is a guy named Tommy in my class, and every time I wear this, my friends say I like Tommy." That was funny, so I inquired more, "Do you like him?" Her blushing was telling me everything, and she giggled and lowered her head. "But Mommy, I don't want him to know that," she said shyly. So, that recollection helped me to completely understand when her girlish ways no longer longed for back braids like her dad had. I was thinking "poor thing" for my husband, that is, because I knew this news was going to break his heart. This kind of little shift in their bond was impacted by something most of us get blinded by as parents, and that is our children's social development. Some parents would rather rush their kids into the pre-teen and adult matters of society in order not to be surprised about their interest and be the ones to shape it, while some parents shield them from the pre-teen and adult matters of society in order to not have to deal with their children's social development and some enjoy the process of letting nature take its course no matter when it occurs because the focus is knowing when nature is moving their children into a new direction. As parents, it is important to have a pulse on our children to guide them as they need it (whether they want it or not). Having a pulse on their social development as nature takes its course can buy us some time to prepare for the inevitable. I realized my husband was not ready for the next stage of our daughter's social development. To walk him through it: I explained to my husband what was going on with our daughter the best way I could, and although he did not openly admit it, he was feeling "some kind of way," but he instantly stated "she was tripping" we laughed and adjusted to her becoming more socially aware and expansive. This met **our opinion and would** no longer be the only thing that influenced her. What others thought of her has now infiltrated her thought life even more, and she did not want to be identified in a way she wasn't, and those styles of braids did just that at the time.

Understanding our child's social development stages when they occur can help us exhibit patience, but it does not exonerate us from parenting. As parents, we think that as long as we provide for our children, we are winning. But during our children's development stages, they will quickly drain us before we can even pat ourselves on the back for paying our mortgage, rent, or any bills in order to provide a stable and consistent home for them. Our children are still developing and could care less about how we believe they are doing well in spite of our hard work. Girls' social development, in particular, in many cultures, was not always accepted so easily back then. Many of us women can relate to this. So of course, it was important that we talked to our children as well as provided for them. I'm happy that I was able to address certain concerns that my daughter had during that time. She was concerned about wearing that outfit. It was my responsibility to talk to my daughter about not allowing people to make her feel bad about what we allowed her to wear; or feel bad about her preferences. Also, how to appropriately respond to bullies and peer pressure. Yes, we, as her parents, have the last word when it comes to how our child represents the family with her style: This reflects on our values, religious preferences, and culture. And having the last word was not surprising to her because this was the norm we developed in our home. We will discuss the importance of shaping your family the way you want it to, more in chapter 5.

"Understanding our child's social development stages when they occur can help us exhibit patience, but it does not exonerate us from parenting."

REFLECTION QUESTIONS

1. In what ways have you observed your child's behavior changing over time?

____

____

____

____

____

2. At what point did you notice a shift in your child's interests or preferences, and how did it manifest?

____

____

____

____

____

3. How did you respond to these changes in your child's behavior or preferences? Did you actively address them, or did you choose to overlook them?

____

____

____

____

____

____

CHAPTER TWO

IT TAKES A VILLAGE

IT TAKES A VILLAGE

It takes a village because life as we know it can take us through some rocky roads and down into some valleys to drop us off in places such as: Divorce, marriage, and divorce again, seeking child support, starting a business, bad dates, rejections, getting fired, looking for employment, finding a new job, stuck in a bad job, miscarriages, and loss of a parent, buying a new home, eviction, going to church, finding a new church, a cheating spouse, you being a cheater, bankruptcy, and more. I know I'm preaching to the choir, but I wanted to acknowledge this and more because, through it all, we still have to raise these kids. Believe it or not, how we deal with our issues is the lens through which our children see things in their adult lives. If we neglect getting help and remain depressed or become bitter, hateful, and unforgiving, so will our child (ren). Being part of the parent squad is a full-time plus job, and you must pay attention at every level; when you can't, because that happens at times, find someone you can rely on that will uphold the standards you have set up for your household.

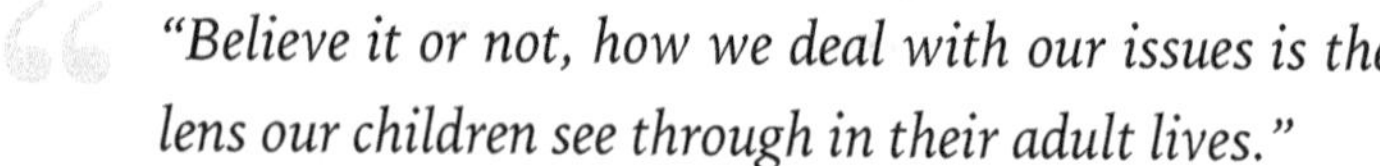

"Believe it or not, how we deal with our issues is the lens our children see through in their adult lives."

Yes, prevention is the key. And that is where my village was born. Because life happens and we have to become each other's village. This is what I did for my siblings, and in return, my parents and siblings did for me. My older brother Jude played a huge part in my daughter's and my "3" nephews' everyday activity lives, especially during the summer, spring and winter breaks. Two of my nephews were his children. He would pick up the kids, and we would donate funds for gas and the activities of their choice. His two boys either stayed with me or my sister during their breaks. During that time, he would teach them an instrument, talk to them about the Bible and teach them church songs. At times, he would process with them how to avoid being in compromising situations. Jude has more flexibility and lives a humble life of service. We are blessed to have him. My husband Earl and I would discuss the kids' activities with them and what they learned and add more perspective to it if need be. Communication is key, and when communication occurs outside of the child being punished or yelled at, rapport can be built. My sister Kathy and brother David were the ones who enjoyed having educational talks with the kids and focused on making sure my daughter and nephews were not just going through the flow of school but actually focusing on learning with excellence. The key is knowing your strengths, and since I was not the classroom teacher type, my husband Earl and I took them to bookstores and spent a lot of time there. We encouraged specific and free learning, played cards, took them to the mall, and my husband taught them how to cook and cooked for them. Earl taught them how to clean and be responsible in ways that would foster maintaining independence.

I was the ordering pizza type mother and aunt and the one who bought those books and workbooks that would prepare them for the next grade level. As my daughter got older, every summer, she had to complete workbooks that would prepare her for the next grade level she was going to, or else she would get into trouble. When it came to me, I was the main one they came to for their social issues, like dealing with their friends, all types of relationships with a boyfriend, girlfriends, making decisions about which club to join and all other life issues. But I knew, and the kids knew as well, to not come to me with any math problems or academic calculative, etcetera. We had my other siblings for that support. My sister Kathy was also the overspending aunt that the kids enjoyed on the main holidays. The point is that as adults, we must know our strengths and weaknesses so we can identify who and where to draw help from. This will allow our children to become well-rounded because every parent will need help sometimes. Making sure you allow your child to get assistance from a trusted adult in the areas in which you are not gifted is key. It will allow you to be less frustrated. My siblings and I took full advantage of each other to assist where we knew our strengths lay. My older sister was the real patient one and also the one who provided more expensive activities. I was the one who provided activities that were more economical and that allowed for family bonding. David and I were both the no-nonsense ones, while Kathy and Jude were the easy-going ones. My parents picked my daughter up from school while we were at work during her primary school stage. And when we needed a date night or a break, my parents kept my daughter for the weekends. It takes a village, but you must ensure that the village is safe for your children.

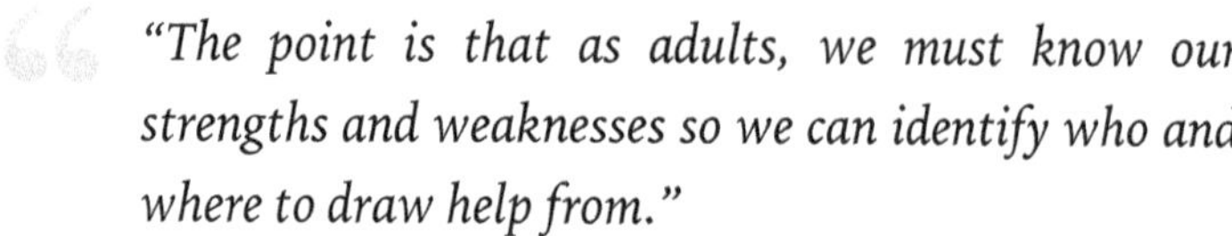

"The point is that as adults, we must know our strengths and weaknesses so we can identify who and where to draw help from."

In some villages, there may be some snakes in the form of individuals we must be careful of. Be prepared by preparing your child to always take precautions. As a social worker, every time I thought I had seen it all, I ended up seeing some more. So, I always prepare my daughter. Transparency with your children will not break them. My daughter was "woken" to her responsibilities to make sure she remained as safe as she could. For instance, me and her biological father were divorced, and I met a wonderful man about six years later and we got married in the month of her 9th birthday. My husband was a single parent of a 14-year-old teenage boy. Because of this, in a loving manner, I assertively explained to my daughter one year before I was married how things would change. I explained to her that she had to lock the door when she entered the bathroom and lock it every time she got dressed in her room. I reiterated what I had taught her previously about her private parts staying private and explained that if anyone tried to touch her in those places, she had to let me know. When we were married, I made it clear that these rules were in place to protect everyone, and we would follow them, too. My stepson was doing the same things I told my daughter. I thank God I had no snakes in my village, but that does not mean I regret preparing her. I hoped for the best on this new journey, but I was prepared to stop the worst in its tracks. This kind of protection in place for your children will foster trust in the relationship as I will discuss the importance of your children feeling safe later. If all else fails, they know their parents have tried. It was not difficult for my daughter to apply the new rules in our new home because these are the same rules she had to apply when she slept at her grandparents' house who always had church folks walking in and out. And anywhere else, she spent the night. Things were not always perfect as my family was blended, and my teenage stepson taught me how it feels to have to deal with mental health issues at home and not just at work. My stepson was oppositional and defiant when it came to following rules. He did not like it, and that affected his education. He was dealing with abandonment issues from his biological mother. So, no matter what we did, he would run away to try to be with his mother, although Children and Families had opposed it in the court of law. Our family and friends helped us with him, too. They kept him some nights, and my sister-in-law Rose, who was also a social worker as well, provided me with a lot of mental health support. I had to become more resourceful and find local agencies that provided counseling and in-patient family therapy. He unfortunately found a loophole and got connected to his mother's side of the family and eventually left the state to stay with his biological mother, and he never got a high school diploma. But as a man, we can talk and unite with him, knowing we tried and we did not let him fail without a fight. We are still praying for him and encouraging him every chance we get.

"I hoped for the best on this new journey, but I was prepared to stop the worst in its tracks."

When prepared, we can carefully build a village that is safe, innovative, and supportive for our child (ren). It is the parents' responsibility to inform their child (ren) of their reality. And everyone's responsibilities are different. We will discuss how and when in the following chapters. I've been a social worker long enough to know that in any relationship, there is no such thing as one-size-fits-all. Your village has to serve your family's reality. If you work at night or twelve-hour shifts, or you are in the military, we are still responsible for making sure your village is safe for your child(ren). So again, I welcome the parent squad to a village and a community where the roads can be rocky, so hold on tight.

REFLECTION QUESTIONS

1. During difficult times, how do you find yourself showing up for your child(ren)?

   a. Do you talk openly with them about what's going on?
   b. Do you reach out to trusted family members or community for support?
   c. Do you sometimes feel overwhelmed and struggle to show up at all?
   d. Are there other ways you've found that seem to work for you and your child(ren)? (Please share)

____

____

____

____

____

____

____

____

____

2. Have you reflected on how changes in your lifestyle—such as introducing new people—might impact your child(ren), either positively or negatively? What thoughts or concerns come up for you?

____

____

____

____

____

3. Have you discussed healthy boundaries with new partners or stepchildren to help create a safe and supportive environment for everyone, especially your child(ren)? What did those conversations look like (or what might they look like)?

____

____

____

____

____

CHAPTER THREE

RAISE THOSE CHILDREN OF YOURS

THREE
RAISE THOSE CHILDREN OF YOURS

The parenting process should begin at home. So many times, I see parents try to implement a structure in public that is not enforced at home. Trust me, everyone can tell! Your child's attitude about your newfound rules in public tells on you. It's like a parent coming to school to punish their child for issues they have never addressed at home as inappropriate. It is always obvious that this is the only time this child is getting any type of real reprimand. Teenagers usually call their parents a "fake" or a "hypocrite" when corporal punishment is being applied at school for others to see. Yes, they are quick to judge and differentiate whether the public shame is because you felt embarrassed or you were actually concerned about them. Whether or not they call you a "fake" or "hypocrite" out loud or to self, it is noted. Some parents do not care, and once they are in private, they openly tell their child to "stop embarrassing me," and they urge their child to get better friends so they can copy what they don't have the time to teach. That part is the harsh reality for a lot of children.

Many parents are understandably confused, and this occurs sometimes when certain things were not enforced on us as a child and, therefore, were not important until the teacher called us. Trust. As parents, most of us can relate, especially when it comes to cultural differences or different religious practices. Sometimes circumstances, like illness in a family, occur that rob us of the time to curtail certain behaviors. Financial priorities to survive can also rob us of the time to teach our children. A shortcut many have used is when you have more than 1 child that are far apart in age. Many parents rely on older children to teach younger ones what is acceptable or not acceptable. When my parents missed opportunities to address certain dos and don'ts, my older sister would also get into trouble. Other times, my parents would say to us rather sternly and with consequences at hand, "I don't know where you got this behavior or attitude from, but you need to go get a refund." That was their way of speed-tracking the talk, saying, "That is not what we do in this family." Now, keep in mind that "speed talks" are more effective if you first do the basics.

Curtailing your child's behavior is mandatory, starting at a very early age. Talking to your child constantly about unacceptable behaviors they exhibit is far more effective than thinking we can just punish our child and the behavior will never occur again. We have to continue to make sure they do not think about putting themselves and us in a bad predicament again. Letting our children know who's in charge should begin in the first 5 years of their life. And believe me, this is the basics. Although it is the most difficult time for us to correct our child's behaviors because, in the first 5 years, they are the cutest, missing that opportunity will make parenting difficult if it hasn't already. It is important to use discipline as an opportunity to teach our child (ren). Asserting discipline will save us from having authority issues as our child gets older because we won't have to deal with behavior issues as much. What's also important is immediate discipline. Deal with it as soon as it happens. Provide immediate consequences for our child's unacceptable behaviors. This is needed when our child misbehaves at an inconvenient time and we are unable to implement punishments at the moment. As parent(s), we must let the child know "that particular behavior was unacceptable" and tell them this at the moment it occurred, and let them know, "We will deal with them later." Dealing with them by talking to them on the ride home can be a conversation about why their behavior was wrong or talking to them first thing in the morning during breakfast.

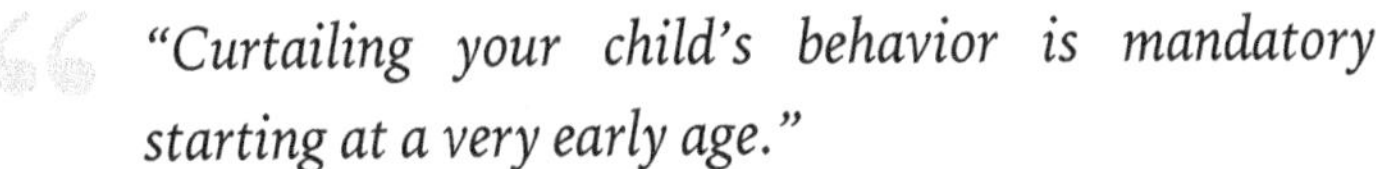

"Curtailing your child's behavior is mandatory starting at a very early age."

Taking the time to correct our child's behaviors is as important as knowing that every child and situation is different. Therefore, as parents, we should implement expectations and respond to their behavior in a proper and suitable way. One method that I found effective is for parents to know what is more important to each child because every child is different, and we need to use those key points to apply precision in curtailing certain behaviors. In certain states, corporal punishment is legal, and in other states, no. In the state I grew up in, corporal punishment was legal, and my dad took advantage of that, but he did not apply it to all of us. Each child had a different method by which they would receive consequences. However, there are some methods that can work for all children if parents apply them with precision.

#1 We ought to brag about what we give them. I say this because most parents are on autopilot and really do not know what to brag about. Knowing the legal requirements for raising a child is key. The law basically says we must provide for the welfare of the child. This would keep them healthy and safe. So, knowing this allows us to punish and not abuse. This means our kids need clothes but not name brand/popular clothes or name brand shoes, etcetera. They need nourishment and not extra things like ice cream and milkshakes. Our golden card to implementing punishments is taking away social media privileges until their homework is completed, of course. Cell phones can be taken immediately, but laptops or desktop computers must be monitored to limit it to schoolwork if your child is being punished. The reality of our financial situation can cause issues when bragging about what we give. Keep in mind that bragging is not limited to material things but to opportunities. As parents, we must be honest with our children and not let them limit our worth to what we can only provide materialistically. This is why we must be active in standing against bullies because that attitude can affect our homes. If they feel like the Reeboks we bought them do not mean much because they are being made fun of and the neighbor has a more expensive brand of shoes our child's attitude can be bitter.

#2 Let children know that they are responsible for keeping the benefits we give them. And if they lose the benefit while being punished, allow them to earn it back quickly. For instance, taking what matters to them can help their perspective on how awesome of a life they do have when those benefits are taken away. For instance, the opportunities to attend parties, or having cell phones, and/or having access to all toys and video games if they behave appropriately and/or chores are done in the allotted time we told them to complete them; then we should give the child those privileges back immediately, especially as noted: When chores are completed, and expected behaviors are met. That will allow us to address those same responsibilities next time by asking, "Am I going to have to take your phone again?" Most children will respond "no" and get moving on what they were told to do or know to do. Depending on the behavior or attitude, keep the punishment going a little longer. Differentiation in how we treat the child who followed the rules and the one who did not follow the rules also helps make our point, and that main point is "a happy mom or dad/nanny is a happy time for you too, little ones."

#3 Let's pick our battles and battle them wisely. There should be a range of differences in how we react when dealing with our child when he or she misbehaves. If everything they do or say is always a "bombshell" reaction, they will become numb to our punishments and reprimands. Over-reacting all the time can induce a depressed child when they constantly feel like everything they do is wrong and they can never make us happy. So, if mental health is an issue personally, we should deal with it. Therefore, if we are overly harsh, and highly emotional, we ought to quickly apologize for our reaction. Continue to be stern about what the reprimand is and lighten up on the punishment if our extreme "overreaction" was clearly punishment enough. This means that, based on how we reacted, that clearly made our child remorseful for that behavior, so why not lighten up on the punishment? Now, if it is the 2nd time or more this child has exhibited that unwanted behavior, we must increase the punishment. Often, we have to be careful not to give our children the wrong message by how we react to them individually in front of each other. For example, the punishment for the child who didn't tie their shoelaces or ate all the peanut butter should not be the same for the other child who steals candy or anything out of a store. This can be tricky because age matters. For instance, if two 5-year-olds eat all the peanut butter, we let them know it's bad (unless they are allergic to peanut butter), but normally, it does not require an extremely harsh scolding. Simply have a conversation and hide the peanut butter. But if 1 child eats all the peanut butter and the other 5-year-old steals money from our purse, there should be a clear difference in our reaction and punishment. If the child who steals money from our purse isn't dealt with more harshly, soon, that child will not see a difference in your purse, my purse, the teachers' purse, etcetera. Now, as previously mentioned, age matters, so if a 5-year-old steals and a 16-year-old steals, our punishment for the 16-year-old must also be different. If we scold and punish that 5-year-old and continuously talk about the unacceptable behavior, most likely, he or she is not the same child at 16 years old stealing. But if our child is stealing at 16 years old because of hunger or greed, help the child get a job and explain to the child how they could use the money earned to buy more food. We will continue to implement acceptable punishments, such as removing the child from extracurricular activities like hanging out with friends, going to the mall, and taking some beloved brand-name clothes and shoes. But if they are stealing items they want like games, clothes, money, etcetera… and they only get caught by us, we should punish them as severely. First and foremost, if the owner of the store will not press charges, go with the child to return all the items taken, which allows them to feel the walk of shame. Then, incorporate the punishments mentioned above, like removing the child from extra-curricular activities like no longer being allowed to hang out with friends and no longer going to the mall (because we know the child can't be trusted). But providing the child with a more productive activity, such as volunteering at a homeless shelter or hospital. In addition, as previously mentioned, take away some beloved brand-name clothes and shoes, but also increase chores. We can also have our child research what could have happened if arrested and have the child write us a report on the research completed. Doing the research together is better because of the bonding experience. This is an opportunity to tell the child how hurt we would be if he or she was locked up and how much we love them. We can also help our children find a job to buy the things they want. Also, we can encourage them to share their story in a safe youth group or with family members who are part of that village to help us keep our children accountable for appropriate behaviors. Also, we should consider providing therapy for our children, especially for behaviors that are red flags. The behaviors you know can affect their future negatively, the behaviors that are out of character, and the behaviors you can pinpoint to the changes that occurred during a family hardship of any kind. This is important because the process of talking to our child about why he or she is behaving a certain way or using the whole stealing example again can lead us to a deeper reason than we originally thought, especially if they have been stealing since he or she was 5 years old but never got caught. #4 There is a safety factor, and that is that kids have to feel safe around us before they can respect us and adhere to our rules.

The safety factor is the **4th** but the most important of them all because numbers 1, 2, or 3 will not work without numbers 4. Many times, when I'm counseling teens, whether they are known to be at risk or not, one of the underlining things their defiance had in common was that they did not respect the authority figure who did not keep them safe. If they were abused and felt neglected in any way, where they had to defend themselves and find their own way to survive, they would not respect us, none-theless follow our rules. And that trust has to be earned all over again. If that is true for the child you're raising, it is best to own up to the errors made as an adult and the parent in that relationship. As adults, we understand that circumstances can occur and that they are out of our control. However, it is imperative not to make the child feel worse than they are already feeling. Always give that child options. For instance, the worst thing that can happen to us as parents is allowing a child to be raised in another home because of the unseen circumstances of divorce or financial hardship. We feel awful, and we have lost control of assuring our child's safety the way we know how. But it happens, and this is why open communication with our children is imperative. When a child prefers to be at one parent's house or the other, find out why.

The best thing you can hear from a child is that it's more fun even though all fun and no responsibilities is not the goal, but the most important is safety precautions. We have to observe and listen if that place that used to be their favorite place changes. We should investigate why, by communicating openly. Asking questions and letting them know they have options because we will fight to keep them safe, and that is the key. Even when my nephews wanted my daughter to sleep over at their home, and she asked, I would let her know she could change her mind at any time. At times, she would, and at times, she did not want to hurt her cousin's feelings by saying no, so I would gladly step in as the "villain" or just the stern parent and lay down the law for her to come home for whatever reason I thought of. She always knew she had options. I would resist even her if she informed me about something that could hurt her or has hurt her, but I thought she should return to that place. It's our job to create that safe space throughout their lives for children to talk to us and inform us when they are not safe but still be vigilant, especially when communications are poor.

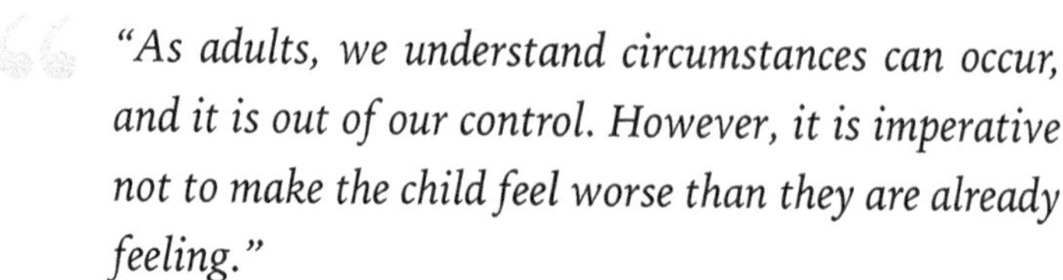

"As adults, we understand circumstances can occur, and it is out of our control. However, it is imperative not to make the child feel worse than they are already feeling."

REFLECTION QUESTIONS

1. Have there been moments when you've noticed behaviors in your child(ren) that felt unacceptable, but you struggled to correct them? What held you back?

____

____

____

____

____

2. Can you recall a time when you felt your reaction to your child(ren)'s behavior may have been more intense than the situation called for? What do you think triggered that response?

____

____

____

____

____

3. Have you ever wondered if your child(ren)'s level of respect toward you is connected to times you felt unable to protect them the way you wanted? How does that impact you?

____

____

____

____

____

____

CHAPTER FOUR

TALK BACK TO ME PLEASE

FOUR
TALK BACK TO ME PLEASE

Yes, we love our child(ren), but our mindset can get in the way of helping our child feel that love. For instance, holding on to certain beliefs that stem from rules that were imposed on us as a child, whether we are aware of it or not, these beliefs will not work. We can be frustrated when our kids have the nerve to talk back. But what is talking back about exactly? In this social media era, today's children just believe they are communicating their minds just as social media have allowed (even when they were not of age to be on social media most children were). Oh, but to some of the traditional parents who grew up in different times and eras, it is considered rude for them to "talk back." Personally, I love children who talk back. It is those quiet children who have actually missed out on our parenting because we made the mistake of interpreting their quietness as obedience, and in return, they are missing out on us addressing wrongful thinking. When a child is not communicating, whether it is considered rude or not, we do not know if we are addressing important issues. It is like responding to a question that was not asked or giving advice about food while someone is having car troubles. We simply do not know in which area that child needs parenting.

And to make matters worse, if that child observes how we react poorly to the child who is talking back or asking questions, most likely, they will not engage with us either. That is because they feel they would be misunderstood, but they will talk about us as a parent and label us to be that parent who is "just not getting it." And they will talk about how their way of thinking is the way to be, therefore, they will start planning on sneaking around to do what they want to do regardless of what the rules are. My parents had a lesson in that while raising their 4 children because me and my younger sibling were the ones who talked back more, and the two older ones didn't. The older siblings were considered very well-behaved children, but the truth is they simply were just quiet. However, my younger brother and I wanted to know why. The "Just because" responses from our parents became old really quick for me. I think this is why I'm not as traditional as my siblings are in general. If something is not working, I stop doing it. During times of conflict with my dad, my mother would have to intervene and talk "to" me and not "at" me, which allowed me to hear her. My father was upset that I had the nerve to talk back, although I was just questioning certain things. But when my mom allowed me to feel heard, I was then able to hear them. Some children are naturally quiet and like I mentioned prior, we have to find a way for them to feel safe to communicate with us as their parents. My daughter would have been the quiet type if I had not consistently forced her to talk and not just talk when she was in trouble. And even then, children don't tell their parents everything. As my daughter got older, she confessed some things to me she kept a secret, and although she is a young adult now, I'm still bracing myself. Some things I knew about but did not tell her, and other things I almost fell out of my chair when I heard of the experiences she had with other adults I trusted with her. Thank goodness she put into place the strategies I taught her to apply, but she chose to keep those experiences to herself at the time.

It is difficult to put our ego aside and start listening to our kids' foolish thoughts when we feel disrespected. But if we listen, it can allow us to find a way to show them how their way of thinking is flawed. But how can we do that if we are not listening? Or are they not talking back? I had an ex-boyfriend once who told me that as a child, he thought that if he cut his fingers, they would grow back. He was astonished as an adult how he really had no fear of losing his fingers because of his perception, which came from watching cartoons a lot. He was adamant about this as a child, but his parents had no idea. This is why having conversations, which was mentioned in Chapter 3, is important. Conversations are not one-sided. Ask questions and wait for an answer. For instance, freely ask that real quiet child, "Sweetie, what were you thinking?" And when he or she responds to your question, go ahead and probe some more, "Why did you believe that?" Identify where the confusion is, and ask questions to ensure the child understood what was said. Sometimes, we do this by giving them a vocabulary test because we sometimes use words they may not understand. At times, we may believe we are being disrespected, but they are also using terms we are unfamiliar with. But continue to ask questions to test their overall understanding of their mishaps and ours. We should not only give our child attention when he/she does something wrong. We would have inadvertently trained them to believe the only way to get our attention is by getting into trouble.

Knowing the difference between when a child is rude and defiant or when a child is just talking back as a form of communication can seem like blurred lines to most parents. To correct our children appropriately means we must listen carefully to what is said and in the context it is being said. We have to want to focus on the bigger issues, and the bigger issue is all about tackling the flawed thought process, which is causing that child to think they know it all. When we strategically show them the errors of their thinking and the consequences, most kids become humble, at least until the next issue arises. When that occurs, you can remind them of the last time they thought they were right. This reminder can help them calm down and listen to us as well as we ought to listen to them. Yes, it is easily written or said depending on the character of the child, but it can be done. Parenting with the concern of trying to teach our child all the things we wish we had known at their age can be stressful. We, at times, make the mistake of telling our children too much too soon, and it comes off as boasting. For instance, if we were always getting arrested this is not something you share unless it appears our child is hanging around questionable people that will cause him or her to be arrested. A strategy to consider is where and how we share that information so it does not come off as boasting, especially about being locked up, unless being locked up is the family's goal. We should focus on all the trauma of being arrested instead (if that is an experience that has to be shared) and how we wouldn't wish that for our child.

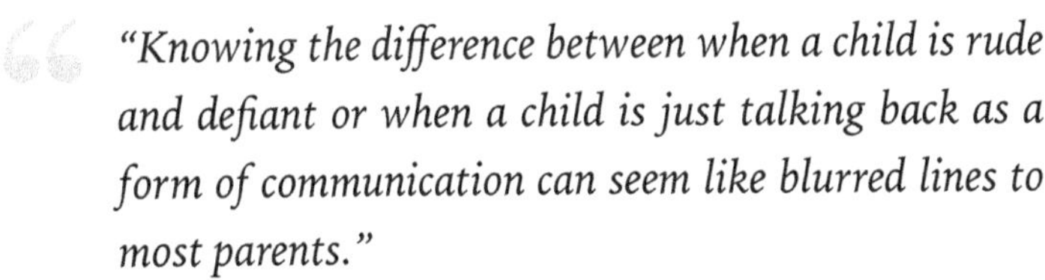

"Knowing the difference between when a child is rude and defiant or when a child is just talking back as a form of communication can seem like blurred lines to most parents."

Being part of the parenting squad means we are actually raising our child(ren), not just watching them grow. It means it is a full-time plus job, and we must pay attention at every level; and when we can't because that happens at times, again, find someone we can rely on that will uphold the standards we have set up for our household. Being part of the parenting squad means we may have to give support at times to other parents' children in order to get support back when we need it for our child(ren).

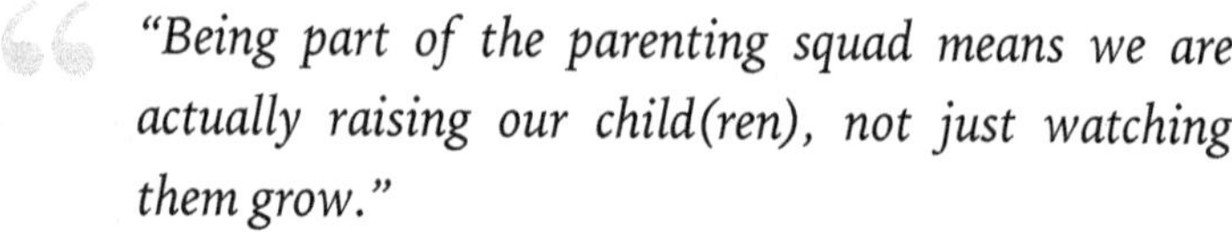

"Being part of the parenting squad means we are actually raising our child(ren), not just watching them grow."

REFLECTION QUESTIONS

1.Looking back on your childhood, what were some wild or surprising thoughts you had that your parents never knew about?

____

____

____

____

____

2. Can you recall a time when you sat with your child(ren), simply listened to them share whatever was on their mind, and asked questions—just to keep listening? What was that experience like?

____

____

____

____

____

3. How often do you find yourself giving your child(ren) attention during moments when they aren't acting out or misbehaving? What does that intentional attention look like for you?

____

____

____

____

____

____

CHAPTER FIVE

THERE IS A PRECISION TO PARENTING

FIVE
THERE IS A PRECISION TO PARENTING

Men come into the parenting squad with a long list of biases already set against them at the door (per se). Mainly because expectations have been traditionally low for men and because mothers are known to do more; as a result, they are being celebrated more than fathers are, even if some mothers are not particularly doing the most. I remember my mom sharing her perspective about the responsibilities and the consequences being sexually active has on females vs. males. Such as: Walking around with a belly, not being able to do a lot of the same activities as your peers anymore, dealing with the shame of not being prepared for the baby and all of the stigmas of being pregnant and not married has. Later, she shared more, telling us what her mother taught her, which started with an "aphorism" my mother and my aunts had among them: "Women have children, not men." They would further explain by telling us how men can easily walk away from the baby or their kids, but we, as women, cannot so easily walk away from our baby. Although my mother's point has truth to it, it can't explain matters of a real parent's heart because my father did not play about his children. In fact, he had a very active role in raising us. A glimpse of this was when I was 11 years old my father took me to a professional bra boutique to purchase my first bra. He was tired of telling my mom that I needed one since I was 10 years old. She seemed too busy to handle it, so he did. I will never forget this very important milestone in my life which was one of so many. Men are not limited by society; only the individual can limit themselves. If a father does not raise the bar like my father did when I needed it, it can be seen as a personal choice and the condition of a bad heart or poor skill, hence shining a light on the saying, "Women have children, not men."

There should be precision in building our own family culture. The journey chosen for your personal family can be more of a spiritual one, or an intellectual, athletic, entertainment or artistic one, but it must be made clear. We as parents will not do well for long trying to trick our children into a lifestyle because they will eventually resent us for it. Initially, basic needs must be met. The basics are nourishment and shelter. Love and open communication about what this family stands for is imperative to building that precision, as we know from the story afforded to us by the Jackson family, A family whose goal was to become famous in the entertainment world. And although the vision was clear it was still a difficult process, so imagine not having clear communication about what the family's vision and goals are. It was difficult not because there was no buy-in but because as children grew, they developed their opinions on "how" to continue to achieve that goal. The Jacksons were known for their musical talents, but eventually, individuals seemed to break free of the limits imposed on them as children, which would not work when they became successful and young teens or adults. Basically, as discussed, "they did change individually." For your family, precision in vision can be for basic things or highly important things. Another family in the public eye that became much more focused on a particular goal and had the buy-in of the whole family is the Wiliams family of Serina and Venus, two very successful tennis players. This allowed for sacrifices to be made where everyone supported the process of these girls' success. I personally utilized precision in raising my daughter and in influencing my nephews in everyday life decisions at different times that would define what we stand for. This kind of precision requires constant communication and open communication. For instance, I recall one of my many conversations with my daughter. As usual, when I picked her up from school, I would ask her, "How was school?" And she would say, "Good," and I would respond by asking, "What was so good about it?" Now, she would talk and talk... and talk... but this was not always the case until I proved much consistency to my inquiries about everything until she was comfortable to just talk without my much inquiry, although I kept my finger on the pulse for changes. This habit led to one of our serious talks that provided a moment for me to get her to buy into it. She was in 2nd grade when she mentioned seeing one of the teachers smoking a cigarette, and I said, "We do not smoke in our family." Now, does that mean I did not have cousins who smoked? No, but in our immediate family, that's just not what we do. Thank goodness that includes my parents, my brothers and my sister as well. My siblings did the same thing in their household when it came to smoking cigarettes, and with other general points, we did not want to have to battle in our households.

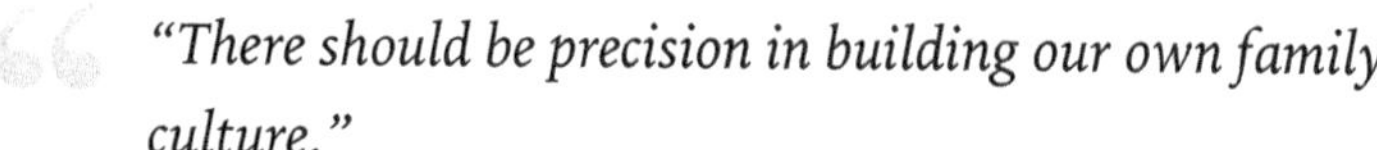

"There should be precision in building our own family culture."

As I mentioned before, you pick and choose how you want to define your family. In our family, our parents' goal was not as extravagant as becoming a world-known athlete or entertainer, but it was just as important, and that was for all of us to have a college degree(s). And all four of us indeed have college degrees, and 3 of us have doctoral degrees. It makes it easier for our children to follow in our footsteps. I recall such an easy path paved for my daughter and nephews to understand that in this family, they did not have a choice but to take education seriously. Especially while they were in grade school, I would tell my daughter that when I was helping her with her homework, in response to "Mommy, I can't," I would say, "What do you mean?" We do not have unintelligent people in our family. Then, I would run through all of our educational accomplishments. By the time my daughter made it to 6th grade, I no longer had to help her or encourage her educationally. She did and turned in her homework all on her own. The importance of education was drilled into her, and as a result, she did well in school. She now has her bachelor's and is getting her master's and aspires to get a doctoral degree. This is also true for a few of my nephews. With every goal, there is a method "to the madness," and that method looks differently depending on where you reside, your race or ethnicity, your family focus and your goals. Just know that it takes precision to raise your child(ren). Parenting should not be done aimlessly without focus and goals. When that occurs, you leave your children open to wandering aimlessly, not knowing the importance of living on purpose. Your child will learn because they are like a sponge absorbing everything around them, so you might as well be the one pouring into them.

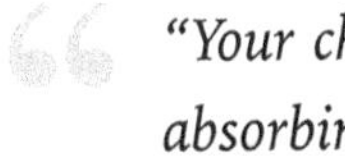

"Your child will learn because they are like a sponge absorbing everything around them, so you might as well be the one pouring into them."

Change is not the enemy, nor does it mean you are a bad parent if your child does not follow through on those family goals when they become an adult or independent. We are here to guide them as parents, not to deny them their destiny. Trust that your precision through hands-on parenting or providing them with a safe environment will work out for their good. I was indeed disappointed initially when my daughter changed her major in college, but I found comfort in her still getting a degree and, most of all, finding her passion. If she aspired to follow her dream, which did not lead to a college degree but had a plan to achieve her goals, honestly, I would be scared a little, but I would still be proud of her. As parents, this may make us feel overwhelmed with worry when they are not staying in line with what we know, but remember, we, too, are learning as we parent. I know it is scary when we do not have a blueprint for success to give our children to follow based on how we define success. But if you guide them in applying a method to succeed, they can use that method for their personal goals that may be different from the family's vision. It just might take longer since that journey with them seems stressful when the path chosen is out of our comfort zone. I remember when I was in middle school, and I was placed in a class as an office aide, but it was with teachers that were with special needs students such as autistic students, intellectually disabled and cerebral palsy students and more. Prior to this, I had never seen students as young as me or around my age under those conditions. I was in shock, and I was overwhelmed with sadness for them, and it mentally paralyzed me during that class period.

I just kept on staring at them, and every chance I could get, I wanted to know what happened. And when they had me run an errand outside of the classroom, I would take my time, hoping for the bell to ring soon. So, today, I am overwhelmed with love and gratitude when my daughter volunteered at an autism center in high school and loved it. She could not stop talking about her clients as if they were her friends. Therefore, when she went to college and changed her major from optometrist to become a behavior analyst, it made sense. What I once could not stomach was the very thing she had a calling to do. I noticed it since she was in preschool when she wanted to be the one to push her classmates' wheelchairs every time her friend needed to be moved. She always enjoyed helping those who needed it. I got a glimpse of it when she was in the 3rd or 5th grade, being happy to be the one to help the teacher with new classmates that came from another country. Every day, she would tell me a new word she had learned in Polish, Spanish or French from her new classmates. See, utilizing precision still allows for space for your child to be free to find their calling in life. If we had not utilized precision while parenting, she would have easily not focused on her responsibility for her future.

A few of the precision buy-ins that worked for us were #1 reminding her that our requirement for her education would be for her benefit. I would ask whose name is going to be on that diploma or degree. Then, we would discuss why these rules were for her benefit. **#2** We would discuss the things that would hinder her from reaching her goals. Things such as promiscuous behavior, drugs, peer pressure, materialism, and watching too much television, etcetera. **#3** Allowing for communication to flow easily when discussing their personal growth and/or hindrances. Maybe because I'm a nosy parent and a therapist, but I wanted to know even the things most people think kids shouldn't tell their parents. My motto has always been if I'm going to end up supporting and helping you through the good times and the bad times, I might as well know the in-between. **#4** When your children know your love is unconditional, they will talk to you even when they become young adults. When this occurs, advice would flow freely both ways because our kids do not remain kids forever, and we, too, would need their advice. For instance, we could ask them to keep us innovative because things change and, as technology advances, we will not always be the best at everything. Parenting with precision allows you to sow in their lives and reap the benefits in ways unimaginable. **#5** Remind them that no matter how successful they think we are, they can help the next generation do better for the next generation to come. I encourage my daughter and nephews to think outside the box. You know that same box their grandparents created for me and my siblings? As parents, we are still growing, so teaching our children to be trainable, respectful, loving, smart, godly and educated individuals, but we need some precision or what others may call "a method to this madness of life." Yet, it is our choice as parents to guide our family until they can guide themselves and the next generation.

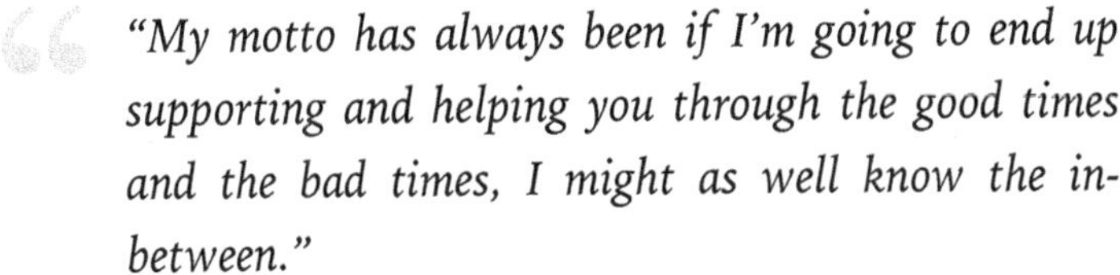

"My motto has always been if I'm going to end up supporting and helping you through the good times and the bad times, I might as well know the in-between."

REFLECTION QUESTIONS

1. Have you taken time to think about and identify the goals you have for your family? What do those goals look like for you?

____

____

____

____

____

____

2. What steps have you taken—or are you willing to take —to help your child(ren) understand these family goals and what they mean?

____

____

____

____

____

3. Do you believe these goals are realistic for your family? How do you feel about the possibility of your child(ren) choosing a different path or having their own goals in the future?

____

____

____

____

____

____

CHAPTER SIX

EVERY DAY, ALL-DAY, JUST SAY IT

SIX
EVERY DAY, ALL-DAY, JUST SAY IT

Anyone can tell you what to do, but it is the journey of being a child, pre-teen, teenager and going into young adulthood that can be difficult. But I want to encourage parents to say something to their children that can make the journey of parenting go smoother. I want us parents to say this until it becomes part of our everyday communication and then as a reminder to our children every moment. This is something I think we do not say enough about, so I am begging. Please tell your kids, "I love you," every day and every time you speak to them. I know in our hearts we do love them, but we don't always feel it when they get on our nerves, and we don't want to say it, especially when their actions at the moment do not match the love we have for them that they happen to push deep, deep, down somewhere. Oh, and we can find it hard to say what was never said to us. So, if we still have the chance, let's practice with them as infants. Say it then, when they are so inno-cent, and our love for them is actually in every breath we take. I know some of us ladies may suffer from post-partum depression. Please seek help. But those of us who don't suffer from postpartum, as we may know already, that love we feel for that infant when they are about 7 lbs, give or take. Our love can eventually seem to be lost in the struggles of life and forgotten momentarily as they grow into pre-teens. It just depends on our life struggles and how soon we stop mindfully realizing we still love that baby of ours no matter how angry they make us. The sun will shine again on that love in our hearts, but in between the temper tantrums, talkbacks, eye-rolling teenagers, and the "know-it-all" young adults, they will make us proud again.

Just saying tell our children we love them may not seem so important, but it is. This is because these children of ours can be downright disrespectful daredevils if they think, even for a second, that we do not "really" love them. They will try us. Some kids understand our guilt for being too busy and know we are buying them off. Some kids will feel bad for us if they understand the reason for our struggle. For instance, telling them, "I love you so much, sweetie. I have to work to make sure I can keep us in this home or get you this and that." Those kid(s) will even go as far as letting us know if we're going too far for some material things. In addition, that conversation about love can foster a well-behaved child. Children have the ability to do anything to be seen or heard, so see them and hear them, and let them know, "We are doing our best because we love you." A child knowing we are on their side and we love them is different from kids who don't know or feel love. For instance, keeping a child away from a parent that presents no harm to them but doing it just because we're upset about the breakup is not showing love to them, nor is trying to recruit that child on our side, which can make it worse. Even if you are trying to keep them safe because you are on their side, it is not enough if you do not explain your love for them. I had to let my child know this even when I was punishing her for something she did, and I'd apologize if I was extra mean, but with love, I still followed through on providing her with the consequences of her poor behavior. As they get older, they understand our rules are not because we are the Grinch of fun days but because we are the concerned, loving parents that they will eventually talk to about their plans versus just hiding them from us. As they grow, they'll take heed of our opinions and advice because they know it comes from a place of love. I believe this will be the result of reminding them every day, when they come home and when they leave for school, to tell them, "I love you" and "Have a nice day, sweetie." So, when you have to emphasize to your child that they need to pick up the phone when you call and remember to do the things you told them to do, they'll understand it's all out of love.

"As they get older, they understand our rules are not because we are the grinch of fun days, but because we are the concerned, loving parents that they will eventually talk to about their plans versus just hiding it from us."

Now, we as parents may have to be relentless in our pursuit to know what is going on in their lives physically and socially, especially on social media. For instance, I was forced to 1st join Facebook, then get a Twitter/X page, next Snapchat, Instagram and finally, TikTok. How else can you track these busy kids(s)? I had threatened to turn off my daughter's phone if she would not pick up when I called, and I even "DM" her on Twitter/X and Instagram, but it worked because she knew it was all out of love. She even provided me with this app to track her so I would not turn off her phone, like I threatened or because she knew I'd keep driving her crazy. She knows I love her because I tell her every day, all day. Some of us are holding on to hurt from our past relationships, and we are taking it out on our children whose father or mother we now hate, but we should focus on shifting the energy on convincing that child or those children of yours how much "no one else wants them to win in life more than we do." Convince them that no one would cry harder for them but us parents if anything bad happened to them. I recall one of my daughter's dear friends had a tough relationship with her mother, and this mother was one of the good ones who worked way too hard and gave her only child everything selflessly. But my daughter's friend was not so appreciative of her mother, so I looked at her while she was trashing her mother and asked her to go talk to her mother. She responded, "Oh please, Ms. Ruth, there is no point." So, I decided to implement the "real talk" therapy method, hoping she would quickly understand me by saying something along these lines: "Listen dear, do you know that no one in this life cares more about you and loves you more than your mother?" "No one will cry harder for you than your mother if something bad happens to you, trust me." I saw the light bulb come on in her mind's eyes, where she lifted her eyebrows, and she started thinking. Well, she did talk to her mother and the maturity of this child has grown since, and their relationship is almost, if not as close as me and my daughter's relationship is. Once your child is convinced, you're their loudest cheerleader, and they know it because you say it and show it, there is not much in this world that can come between that bond. I started telling my daughter, "I love you," when she was an infant, but I had to make her understand the debt of my love from the moment she began talking back at the age of 7 years old. She wanted to listen to her friend's advice and not do her homework, so I asked her, are your friends going to come and suffer the consequences with you? I believe I momentarily entered the twilight zone or traveled into space because I surely was seeing stars. When my daughter said to me, "She is my friend, and no one is going to take me away from my friend." Yes, I had to buckle down and insert homework rules until that child did not want to come over to my house anymore, and eventually, she was mean to my daughter at school. And I was thankful for this necessary wrong that I don't regret occurring. And when things shifted like most relationships do at that age, I was there for her, to prove to her why she had to listen to "mommy" who wanted her to do well, and not fail like one friend in particular did because she was not listening to her own mother. This all occurred at the age of 7, while my daughter was in 2nd grade. I seized the moment and kept my finger on the pulse of what was happening in her life and her friends' lives. If I had missed that opportunity, maybe I could have been dealing with a whole different kind of child today. Who knows? But there will be plenty of opportunities to make your "I love you" mark, all day, every day; just say it to those kids of ours, especially, because it softens life's ups and downs, and with all its twists and turns when we start our day parenting by saying: "I love you," to our children.

Letting our children know that our love is real means a lot, and saying it is the first step towards accepting each other's flaws. Knowing we mean well can go a long way. However, we now have to take the time to understand the conflict that we may have when raising them. It is clear we can mean well, but there is a difference in how we see the world across generational lines, and we have to learn from one another. While our children are young, we have to make sure we are effective in protecting them, and as they grow, we can slowly let them understand the reasons why we did what we did, helping them understand our point of view. This is better for adolescence, after obedience has been achieved. It is okay to obtain obedience in the midst of agreeing to disagree for a time period. For instance, we as parents may know something about the parents of our child's friend, but we can't divulge what we know or how we know it to our children as of yet. But as parents, because we know what we know, we cannot allow our child to go on a trip or have a sleepover with that family. This is why letting our children know we love them goes a long way when we can't share the reasons why we make certain decisions. We must simply ask them to trust us.

Many times, it's not what we say, but how we say it, that leads to constant conflict with our children. Additionally, innovation has played a significant role in complicating the way we communicate. Because we come from different generations, it often feels as though we're speaking different languages, further confusing the meaning of what we're trying to express to one another.

The Baby Boomer generation and the generations prior had very little to no experience with the current speed of technology today. But even Generation X and the Millennials of a certain economic status have not been exposed to or relied on technology the way Generation Z and some of the Millennials have. Because of this, many from the older generations tend to offend our children when correcting them. It's not so much a lack of obedience, but rather the offense that makes the relationship rocky because of the way we relay information. The main reason for this gap in our communication is social media. Previous generations had to spell everything out to us. Those of us who had Baby Boomer parents or were raised by grandparents of the Silent Generation were told more things to increase our social interactions. For instance, they would easily tell us to lose weight, how to eat, and what not to do openly. For this reason, parents from Generation X and some Millennial parents may offend our children without knowing it. Although we love them, they are just so tired of how we continue to openly display things about their flaws. And the reason is that they are exposed to negativity on social media every day. Their access to information is in their back pockets, and as they try to compete with the world and measure up to everyone online, they do not want to feel that their parents are another thing to deal with.

Think about it! Previous generations were slowly exposed to social media, but Generation Z and some Millennials were practically born with a computerized phone in their hands. So, when the previous generation of children felt that they were smarter and more innovative than their parents, they really just felt misunderstood. But this next generation is probably more correct in their assumptions of being more informed because of their access to infor-mation on social media that we did not have and therefore are not as addicted to as they are. Even if parents of Generation X and Millennials have an addiction to social media, we are not influencer followers as our children are.

They are exposed to more things before they can learn the strategy to try to measure up or have to deal with the fact that they will never measure up. So, yes, they are more sensitive and more aware of their feelings. They are smarter at their current age than we ever were at that age. So, part of loving them is not repeating the hurt that they experience every time they get online. Every time they look at their phone—which is a lot—we have to get on social media, follow who they follow, and know what they are being exposed to, letting them know they are enough just as they are. It is a different kind of method, but it is still love. When you can't beat the technology race, join them. Send them positive things online to battle all the negative things that are online. Use technology to your advantage in order to communicate better and in a more loving manner, even when teaching them things that they were not open to when speaking to them. Depending on our ages as parents, saying "I love you" can also be done more innovatively than the previous generations did with us.

REFLECTION QUESTIONS

1. When was the last time you looked your child(ren) in the eye and said, "I love you," just because-without it being a holiday, birthday, or special occasion? How did that moment feel?

____

____

____

____

____

2. In what ways have you challenged yourself to become more creative or innovative in how you connect and engage with your child(ren)? What's worked so far?

____

____

____

____

____

3. What have you learned about the differences between your parents' generation, your own, and your child(ren)'s generation? How has that understanding influenced the way you communicate and strengthen your relationship with your child(ren)?

____

____

____

____

____

____

ACKNOWLEDGMENTS

I would like to express my deepest gratitude to all those who have helped and supported me throughout the journey of writing this book. Without their encouragement, guidance, and unwavering belief in me, this project would not have come to fruition.

First and foremost, I want to thank my mother, Mrs. Esther Doriscar, who displays tremendous strength even when moving in silence. Mommy, you are a well-rounded supporter—I love you now and always.

To my late father, Rev. Woolly J. Doriscar, your strength, leadership, care, and dedication as a protector of our family, alongside your teamwork with my mother, have shaped me and our family into who we are today. Our agreements and disagreements are all to be honored and cherished.

To my daughter, Mrs. Rebekah Hannah—my daughter, my friend, and the one who jogs my memory and keeps it real with me—I love you to the moon and back. Thank you for being honest about your experience with me as your mother.

To my husband, Mr. Earl Cook, thank you for your love, patience, and understanding. Your support has been my rock, and I am truly blessed to have you in my life.

To my older brother and friend, Pastor Jude Doriscar—my personal bishop—thank you for ushering me forward and encouraging me in what you know and believe God has for me.

To Dr. Katsia Cadeau and Dr. David Doriscar, my siblings whom I see as perfectionists and whose dedication is truly inspiring—thank you, David, for telling me, "I have to write this book." Thank you all for believing in this project and helping bring it to readers everywhere. Your professionalism and support have made this journey so much easier.

Lastly, to my readers—thank you for taking the time to read this book. I pray that you find it enthusiastic, supportive as a parent, and that your interest inspires me to keep writing.

This book is not just the result of my effort but the combined influence of everyone I've mentioned and many more. I am forever grateful for your contributions and encouragement.

Thank you all.

With heartfelt appreciation,

    Dr. Ruth Doriscar-Cook

ABOUT THE AUTHOR

Dr. Ruth has been a dedicated social worker since 1997. She holds a bachelor's and master's degree in social work, as well as a doctorate in education. With 26 years of experience, she founded *Living in Victory LLC* to empower individuals on their path to success.

She is also a proud member of the International Society of Female Professionals.

Dr. Ruth is happily married and a devoted mother to her daughter.

SOCIAL MEDIA:

#TheParentSquad

instagram.com/victoryisliving

facebook.com/Victoryisliving

x.com/VICTORYLIVIN

tiktok.com/@victorylivin

threads.net/@victoryisliving